Embrace Your Boundaries With Confidence

Written by Natasa Vella

Illustrated by Daryna Zghurovets

Embrace Your Boundaries With Confidence © Natasa Vella 2025

The moral rights of Natasa Vella to be identified as the author of this work have been asserted in accordance with the Copyright Act 1968.

First published in Australia 2025 by Natasa Vella.
Illustrations by Daryna Zghurovets

ISBN: 978-1-7638584-0-4 (Hardback)
ISBN: 978-1-7638584-1-1 (Paperback)
ISBN: 978-1-7638584-2-8 (E-book)

Any opinions expressed in this work are exclusively those of the author and are not necessarily the views held or endorsed by Natasa Vella.

All rights reserved. No part of this publication may be reproduced or transmitted by any means, electronic, photocopying or otherwise, without prior written permission of the author.

 @the.helicopter.mum

 The Helicopter Mum

Disclaimer

The content, methodologies, competencies, and ideas presented in this publication are intended solely for general informational purposes and should not be interpreted as personalised guidance. This publication seeks to provide a wide array of insights and alternatives, recognising the varied situations and viewpoints of its audience. Any choice to implement the information provided is entirely at the reader's discretion and responsibility. The author and publisher explicitly deny any liability for outcomes, including but not limited to business, financial, personal, or other outcomes, resulting from the application of this material. It is strongly recommended that readers obtain independent professional advice that is customised to their individual circumstances prior to making decisions based on this content.

Dear Alexis and Mason,

This book is dedicated to both of you, with all my love and pride for the remarkable individuals you are becoming.

Alexis, at just 8 years old, you possess wisdom far beyond your years. You are brave and resilient, with an incredible capacity for love, care, and humour. Your kind heart shines brightly, and your willingness to embrace challenges and always "give things a go" inspires me endlessly. Whatever you set your mind to, you can and will achieve—I believe in you wholeheartedly!

Mason, even at 5 years old, your big and bright personality lights up every room. Your kind heart and profound capacity for love are truly extraordinary. You are such a wonderful boy, always going above and beyond to bring joy to others and reminding those around you how cherished they are. Your determination and strength are boundless, and I know you will achieve amazing things. Always stay true to yourself—never feel the need to change to fit in, because you are perfect just the way you are.

With all my love, Mum xXx

Your body and it only belongs to you, knowing your boundaries and keeping yourself safe will empower you. Always listen to your intuition as it knows best. It is our second brain to alarm and keep us safe. Follow these few simple rules to guide and educate you, on how to protect yourself when you get caught in the blue.

Come on, turn the page, so you can learn, grow, and rock your boundaries with confidence.

In case you did not know, our intuition is our superpower, a natural ability that allows us to understand and sense something without needing proof. So, when you are unsure of something new and you have no grown-up near to support you, lean towards your superpower and let your intuition guide you.

Let us talk about the powerful word, NO! Never be afraid to say no, when you are faced with something that makes you feel uncomfortable.

It is perfectly fine to change your mind while playing with your friends, and you decide not to play or share your toy anymore. Saying no to sharing or opting out of a game is completely fine if you are not in the mood.

Remember, you should never feel pressured to do anything against your will. You are a strong and independent individual, and your voice matters. So, if you do not want to do something, no, truly means no. Always respect yourself and others.

Finding your voice can enable you to advocate for yourself and your values, which are incredibly important for guiding and motivating those around you. When you share your thoughts and feelings, you have the potential to inspire others.

We all desire to fit in and feel a sense of belonging. Navigating friendship groups can be challenging, but treating others the way we wish to be treated is a great starting point for being a good friend. It is important to be kind, respectful, helpful, caring, and uplifting.

True friends lift each other up and make each other feel good about themselves. If a friend stops making you feel valued and no longer shows those wonderful qualities, it may be time to prioritize your well-being and step back from that friendship.

Everyone has their ups and downs, but if the negatives start to outweigh the positives, it might be time to seek out new friends who share your beautiful values.

Be kind, and respectful, and incredible things will happen.

Your imagination is a beautiful thing and just the beginning of incredible things

Playing is something we all enjoy; it brings us joy and helps us learn and grow. It is important to remember that play takes team effort, so we should always make sure that everyone involved is having a good time.

If we see that our friend is feeling uneasy about the play, it is important to stop and reassess the game. Taking turns and switching games to suit everyone is a great way to ensure that our playtime remains fun, respectful and enjoyable for all.

*Hold your head high, be courageous,
and continue to let your light shine*

We all love secrets, as secrets can be a lot of fun, especially when they lead to exciting birthday surprises fun! These kinds of secrets are safe secrets, delightful and bring a warm, fuzzy feeling to our tummy and hearts. However, there are also harmful secrets that should never be kept away. These secrets can make us feel uncomfortable, uneasy, and just not seen.

If someone tells you to keep something to yourself, and it just does not sit right, remember that there is always someone special and trustworthy in your life with who you can talk about.

It is completely normal to feel scared about sharing, but just keep in mind how deeply you are loved and that there is always a way to navigate through any challenges. You should also feel proud of yourself for opening up about secrets that should not be kept away.

You are brave, strong, kind, and never be afraid to stand up for yourself.

It is important to have open and honest conversations about our genitals, which are private parts of our body, the vagina, vulva, penis, testicles, and anus. While these body parts often have playful nicknames, it is important to refer to them by their proper names, just as we do with other parts of our body, such as the heart, brain, arms, legs, and lungs.

Using the correct terms helps avoid confusion especially when talking about our bodies. Remember, privacy is key; we should never show, look, or touch someone else's genitals unless it is necessary, such as during a doctor's visit.

If someone tries to touch you or show you their genitals, it is important to speak up loudly and firmly to let them know it is not okay. Always use the correct terms to explain what you have seen or experienced to a trusted adult.

*So, let's go.
Rock your boundaries with confidence.*

Superhero Safety Network activity

Name and colour in the five amazing superheroes. These superheroes make up your very own Safety Network. A Safety Network is made up of caring adults that you can count on. People who are easy to reach, always ready to listen, who believe in you, and are willing to help whenever you need them. These superheroes are here to keep you safe and lift you up, no matter what! By having at least five trusted people in your life, you can be sure that there is always someone ready to listen and support you.

About the Author:

My name is Natasa Vella, I am a proud mother of two wonderful children and with a background in Psychological Sciences and Criminology, I am deeply passionate about promoting children's mental health and well-being, with a strong focus on emphasizing their safety and security. My mission is to help educate the next generation on self-love and acceptance while cultivating environments where they feel valued, empowered, heard, and supported. Together, through continuous learning and engagement with literature, we can grow and refine our practices to support our children better every day.

A note for parents, caregivers, and educators:

Educating children about the importance of healthy and respectful boundaries is essential for their growth and development. Establishing these boundaries early on helps foster and sustain positive relationships, safeguards mental health, and prevents issues such as burnout and resentment. This foundation enables children to grow into resilient, confident, kind, and independent teenagers and adults. Without clear boundaries, individuals may feel overwhelmed, stressed, or taken advantage of, often struggling to manage their time and energy effectively. By instilling a strong understanding of boundaries in the next generation, we empower them to navigate life and relationships with confidence, cultivating a healthier and more balanced approach to both personal and social well-being.

www.ingramcontent.com/pod-product-compliance
Lightning Source LLC
Chambersburg PA
CBRC091724070526
44585CB00008B/167